I0089920

All by Myself

MEGAN AND SIMON

All By Myself

© 2025 Dr Simon Robinson

All rights reserved. No part of this publication may be reproduced, stored in a retrieval system, or transmitted in any form or by any means—electronic, mechanical, photocopying, recording, or otherwise—without the prior written permission of the author.

The right of the author to be identified as the creator of this work has been asserted in accordance with the Copyright, Designs and Patents Act 1988 (United Kingdom).

ISBN: 978-1-0684310-4-3

Printed and bound by IngramSpark

First published in the United Kingdom (2025)

Set in Alex Brush, EB Garamond, Playfair Display, Noto Sans Oriya and Spectral licensed under the SIL Open Font License v1.1.

Page design and layout by Dr Simon Robinson.

Illustrations created by Dr Simon Robinson with the assistance of Chat GPT. or from open source libraries. All images are original compositions used under educational and editorial fair-use principles. Trademark Notice:

All brand names and product references (including Amazon, YouTube, McDonald's, and others) are used for identification purposes only. They are the property of their respective owners and are used under fair and descriptive use principles. No endorsement or affiliation is implied.

This book was written for and inspired by Megan, whose enthusiasm and conversation brought these stories to life.
This publication is designed for educational and developmental use. It is not a medical, psychological, or therapeutic guide.
A copy of this book has been deposited with the British Library in accordance with UK legal-deposit requirements.

For further information visit:

drsimonrobinson.com | wordbotherers.com

WB

GROUP OF AUTHORS

One day,

I'll be able to do it,

all by myself

— I'm not scared

MEGAN, AGED 24

CONTENTS

Introduction   7

All by Myself   9

Cities   11

Water   15

Gas   17

Being Polite   19

Maths   21

Turquoise   27

Double and Half   35

Galaxies   43

Percentage   47

Politics   49

Geometry   53

Candles   59

Walking to College   63

The Mind   65

Want and Need   69

Amazon   73

Animals   75

Pat's Temporary Accommodation   83

Doing My Laundry   87

MEGAN & DEXTER

INTRODUCTION

The primary purpose of this book is to help Megan develop her understanding of concepts and the building blocks of all concepts, words.

We began simply, with learning cards: small emoji pictures paired with printed words. From these, Megan learned to associate symbols with meaning. Later, we introduced short printed sentences, which she memorised long before she could truly read them. Gradually, those familiar combinations of words became recognisable in new contexts — the first steps of genuine reading.

To build on this progress, we created *A Little Bit of Help* — a collection of short stories written with Megan, featuring words and ideas already familiar to her. Because these stories reflected her own experiences, they became a natural point of reference. We read them together several times a week, using each repetition to reinforce her understanding and strengthen her confidence.

Now, we are ready to take the next step. *All By Myself* continues the journey, exploring a new layer of concepts that point towards independence, understanding personal safety, practical routines, and the confidence to navigate daily life.

At the end of this book, I have included an appendix of lists and tables. These are designed to encourage further development through curiosity, helping Megan (and others like her) to deepen their familiarity with the words, patterns, and relationships that shape the world around them.

ALL BY MYSELF

Mum, Dexter and me went walking to our local shop.

I wasn't scared, even though there were people shopping.

Mum kept an eye on me — ***all by myself.***

One day, I'll be able to do it, ***all by myself*** — *I'm not scared.*

And one day, when I understand more, I'd like to be able to **drive a car.**

I'm learning, more and more.

👑 **Edinburgh**

Newcastle

Leeds

Sheffield

Scotland

Northern Ireland

North East

North West

York & Humber

Belfast 👑

Liverpool

Manchester

Birmingham

East Midlands

West Midlands

Wales

Anglia

Cardiff 👑

South West

South East

Bristol   **London** 👑

CITIES

"Okay, Megan, remember when we talked about towns and villages?" asks Simon.

"Why do we say those words?" Megan replies.

"*Good question* — but I asked you a question..." says Simon.

Villages are places where there are only a few houses, and maybe just one shop or pub.

Towns are places where there are hundreds, maybe thousands, of houses and lots of shops, a few schools, and maybe a hospital. Sometimes they even have a railway or bus station if they are big towns.

Cities are places where there are thousands of houses, a railway and bus station, many schools, and several hospitals.

The most important city in each country is called the capital city.

FACTS ABOUT THESE CITIES

EDINBURGH

Capital of Scotland. Famous for its castle on the hill and the big arts festival called the Edinburgh Festival.

LEEDS

A large city in Yorkshire. Famous for shopping, universities, and its history in the wool trade.

NEWCASTLE

A city in the north of England. Known for its bridges across the River Tyne and the football team Newcastle United.

SHEFFIELD

Once called the "Steel City" because it made a lot of steel. Today it is known for music and green parks.

BELFAST

Capital of Northern Ireland. Famous for building the ship Titanic and for its colourful wall murals.

BIRMINGHAM

Second largest city in the UK. Famous for canals, factories, and the Bullring shopping centre.

LIVERPOOL

A port city in northwest England. World-famous as the home of The Beatles.

CARDIFF

Capital of Wales. Known for Cardiff Castle and the Millennium Stadium for rugby.

MANCHESTER

Known for its football teams Manchester United and Manchester City. It was also a centre of the Industrial Revolution.

BRISTOL

A port city in southwest England. Famous for the Clifton Suspension Bridge and hot air balloons.

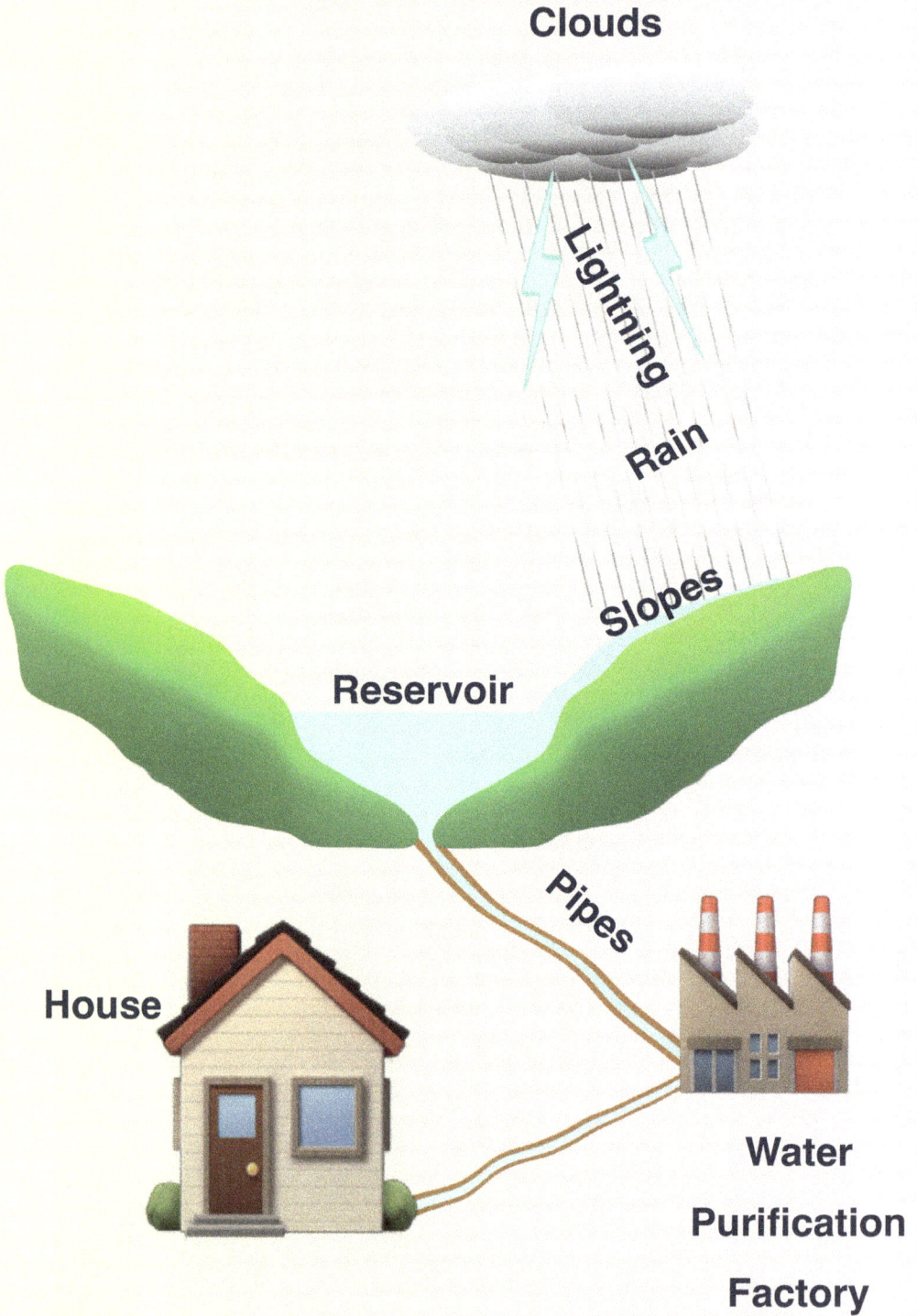

Clouds

Lightning

Rain

Slopes

Reservoir

Pipes

House

Water
Purification
Factory

WATER

"Where does water come from, Megan?" asked Simon.

"*From the kitchen,*" Megan replies, giggling. "*From the tap!*"

Water falls from the sky as rain.

This rain runs down the slopes into the brooks and rivers.

Then the rivers flow to the sea.

We catch and store the rain in **reservoirs**.

This water is cleaned in a **purification** factory and then travels in pipes to our houses.

The **pipes** bring the clean water to our taps.

"Does this make sense?" asked Simon.

"Yes," said Megan.

💧 VOCABULARY BOX

Reservoir – a large lake made by people to store water.

Purification – cleaning something to make it safe.

Pipes – long tubes that carry water or gas.

GAS

We have been learning about gas.

Gas is **invisible**. This means we cannot see it, but...

We can smell it — *it stinks*.

We can hear it as it comes out of the cooker — *it hisses*.

We have to **be careful with gas** because it is:

🔥 **Flammable** — it can catch fire.

💥 **Explosive** — it can blow up.

🚑 **Dangerous** — it can hurt you.

We use gas that comes in pipes for cooking and heating water. We need hot water for showers and to warm up the **radiators**.

"I'm not yet allowed to use the cooker. For the moment I am just learning how to be safe," said Megan.

🔥 VOCABULARY BOX

Invisible – something you cannot see.

Flammable – can catch fire easily.

Explosive – can blow up with a bang.

Radiators – heaters on the wall that make a room warm.

BEING POLITE

When we are outside the house, it's important to learn how to be **polite.** If we just behave as we want, this might be seen as **rude.**

"I'm not knocking at your bedroom door this morning, am I?" says Megan.

"Yes — you are learning how to be polite! These are important rules if you don't want to be seen as rude."

So, you have learned to wait until we are awake before knocking at our bedroom door. *Excellent!*

You have also learned not to **interrupt** conversations but to wait for your turn.

Today we talked about **gossiping** — this means talking about things you hear that are nothing to do with you. This is hard because we all want to gossip when we have heard something interesting. But if we want to be polite and not rude, we must *try not to gossip.*

🗣 VOCABULARY BOX

Polite – showing good manners, being kind and respectful.

Rude – the opposite of polite, behaving in a way that upsets others.

Interrupt – to stop someone speaking by talking over them.

Gossip – talking about other people's business when it's not yours

MATHS

"Have you heard about **maths**, Megan?"

"Why do we have to talk about **maths**?"

"*Good response.* Maths is all about using **numbers**. A few hundred years ago, when people didn't know much about maths, they thought it was **magical**. Today, we need and use maths everywhere — for counting money, using computers, building things, and much more!"

"What can we do with numbers then?"

We can use them to count things.

✚ Adding

We use adding to count quickly.

If we have a £20 note, a £10 note, and a £5 note, we can add **£20 + £10 +£5** to find we have £35.

— Take Away

We use take away (subtracting) to find how much is left when we pay for things.

For example, if our shopping costs £35 and we pay with two £20 notes (**£20 + £20 = £40**), then we take away **£40 − £35 = £5** change.

✖ MULTIPLY

If we need to count many things, we use multiplication.

If we had four £10 notes, we can multiply **4 × £10 = £40.**

Learning multiplication tables helps us add up quickly.

CALCULATOR

VOCABULARY BOX

Maths – the study of numbers, shapes, and patterns.

Add – to put numbers together to make a bigger number.

Take away (subtract) – to find out how much is left.

Multiply – to add a number to itself many times.

Change – the money you get back after paying too much.

THE TEN TIMES MULTIPLICATION TABLE

Number	times	ten	equals	answer
1	x	10	=	10
2	x	10	=	20
3	x	10	=	30
4	x	10	=	40
5	x	10	=	50
6	x	10	=	60
7	x	10	=	70
8	x	10	=	80
9	x	10	=	90
10	x	10	=	100

TURQUOISE

Simon needed to buy a new car. The **black Peugeot** was over eighteen years old, which is very old for a car. Simon and Pat went to some of the car **showrooms** in Scarborough.

"I thought we were getting a **white** car," said Megan.

But when I came home, there was a different coloured car where the white car should have been.

At first this *stressed me out!* But when Simon explained, *I calmed down.*

This **turquoise** car was just for a few days until the white car was ready.

I was glad that I learned that understanding helps me calm down and not get stressed, because guess what? Simon had another car — a **black** Astra — which the garage gave him while they finished sorting out the white car!

🎨 VOCABULARY BOX

Turquoise – a bright blue-green colour, like the sea.

Peugeot – a French make of car.

Showroom – a place where cars are displayed and sold.

New Colours!

Navy

A very dark blue, like the colour of the night sea.

Lavender

A pale purple, softer than pink or purple.

Peach

A soft, pale pink-orange like the fruit.

Olive

A green with hints of brown or yellow, like olives.

Navy Jumper

Lavender Bobble Hat

Peach Briefcase

Olive Van

Turquoise Umbrella

Beige Shorts

Teal Top Hat

Maroon Car

Turquoise

Blue-green and vibrant, often associated with oceans and gems.

Beige

A light, sandy brown, common in clothing and walls.

Teal

A deep, rich green-blue, often confused with turquoise.

Maroon

A deep reddish-purple, darker than red.

THE TWO TIMES TABLE
- USED FOR DOUBLING

How many	times	two	equals	answer
1	x	2	=	2
2	x	2	=	4
3	x	2	=	6
4	x	2	=	8
5	x	2	=	10
6	x	2	=	12
7	x	2	=	14
8	x	2	=	16
9	x	2	=	18
10	x	2	=	20

DOUBLE AND HALF

"What does '**double**' mean?" Megan asks.

"'Double' means to make something twice as big.

If I said I want two bars of chocolate, and then changed my mind and said, '*Double this!*' it means I now want four bars of chocolate."

Double (times two) of two equals four.

So when we double something, we multiply it by two.

$$🍏🍏 × 2 = 🍏🍏 + 🍏🍏$$

$$= 🍏🍏🍏🍏$$

✖ Double

Double of £10 is:

$10 \times 2 = £20$

📘 Vocabulary Box

Double – to make something twice as big (×2).

Half – to split something into two equal parts.

Third – to split something into three equal parts.

Quarter – to split something into four equal parts.

Pair – two things that go together (like shoes or gloves).

÷ HALF

When we 'half' something we divide it into two equal parts.

If we *want to share* one cake between two people each person gets 1/2 each.

$$\tfrac{1}{2} + \tfrac{1}{2} = 1$$

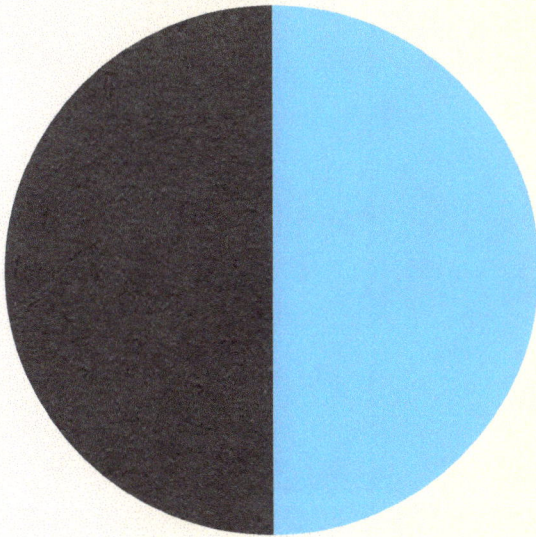

÷ Third

When we '**third**' something we divide it into three equal parts.

If we want to share one cake between three people each person gets 1/3 (a third) each.

$$\tfrac{1}{3} + \tfrac{1}{3} + \tfrac{1}{3} = 1$$

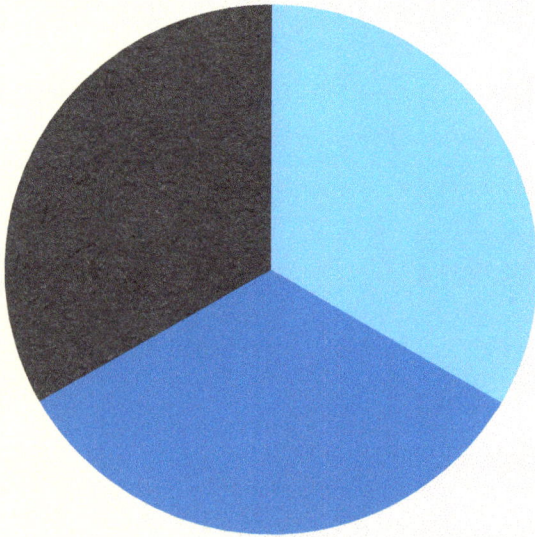

÷ QUARTER

When we '**quarter**' something we divide it into four equal parts.

If we want to share one cake between four people each person gets 1/4 (a quarter) each.

$$¼ + ¼ + ¼ + ¼ = 1$$

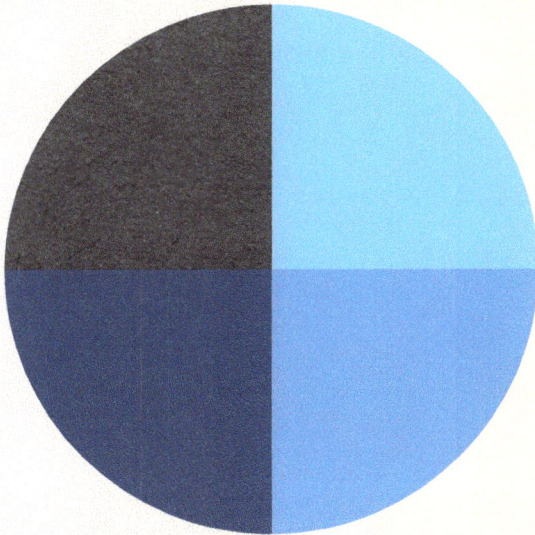

👠 PAIRS OF SHOES

Shoes (and socks and gloves) are bought in **pairs**.

If we have three pairs of shoes and somebody asks, "*How many shoes?*"

3 pairs × 2 = 6 shoes.

That's the ***same as doubling!***

BOOTS

PAIRS OF THINGS

hands

jeans

gloves

glasses

socks

flip flops

boots

shorts

chopsticks

skis

roller boots

skates

ballet shoes

maracas

drumsticks

crutches

scissors

NASA/ESA Hubble Space Telescope
image of colliding galaxies.

GALAXIES

Simon was watching a YouTube video about outer space.

"*What's that?*" asked Megan, pointing at the television.

"That is a **galaxy**," said Simon.

Galaxies are made up of many, many **stars**.

Stars are like the **sun**, only they are much further away, so they look like tiny points of light.

"Why do we talk about the **moon** and the stars?" asks Megan.

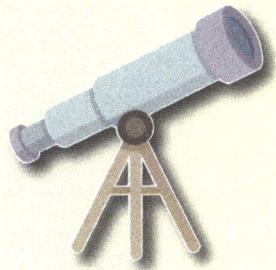

TELESCOPE

"Remember yesterday when you asked what a galaxy was?"

"Yes."

"Well, before you can understand what a galaxy is, you start with the moon and stars.

We live on a planet we call **Earth**. This is like a really big ball that we live on. Don't worry, we won't fall off, because gravity sticks us to Earth. *Try jumping off it!*"

The moon is a smaller ball of rock that travels around Earth in a loop called an **orbit**. It is the closest thing to Earth in outer space.

Earth is one of eight planets. All these planets orbit the sun.

The sun is a very, very, very big ball of hot fire. It gives us light (during the day) and keeps us warm.

All the planets and their moons orbit the sun, and together we call this the **Solar System.**

And the Solar System is just one of many. All the solar systems and their suns are in a big group called a galaxy.

The name of our galaxy is the *Milky Way.*

IMAGE
Created by NASA and ESA. NASA Hubble material (and ESA Hubble material prior to 2009) is copyright-free and may be freely used as in the public domain without fee, on the condition that only NASA, STScI, and/or ESA is credited as the source of the material.

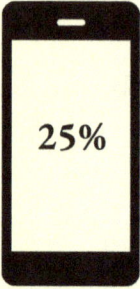
25%

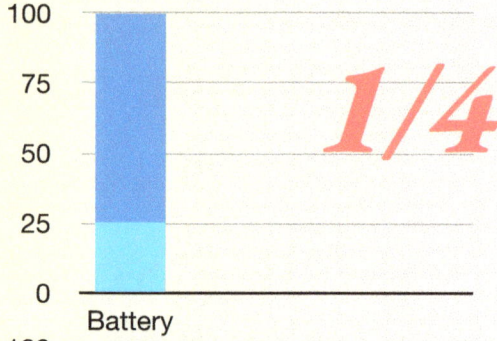
100
75
50
25
0
Battery
1/4

50%

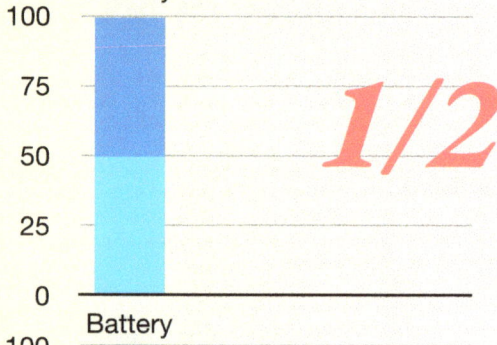
100
75
50
25
0
Battery
1/2

75%

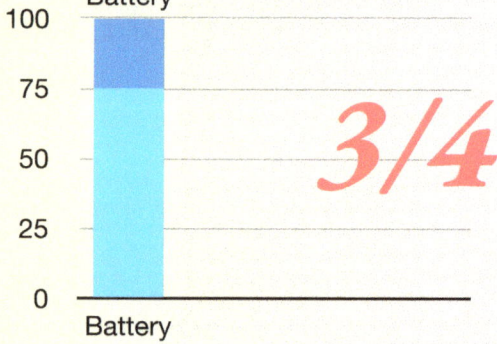
100
75
50
25
0
Battery
3/4

100%

100
75
50
25
0
Battery
Full!

PERCENTAGE

"Hey Megan, have you heard of **fifty** percent (**50%**)?"

"This means the same as **half** — ½."

When your phone battery is **full**, it says **100%.**

When your phone battery is **half full**, it says **50%.**

And when the battery is almost **empty**, the percentage goes down towards **0%.**

"What does '*percent*' mean?"

It means per hundred. *It's tricky now, but you'll soon understand.*

BIG BEN

UNION JACK

THE HOUSES OF PARLIAMENT

POLITICS

"What is **politics** about, Megan?"

"*I don't know,*" she replies.

In every town and city, there are people who help make the **laws** — the rules that we all must follow.

Every four years or so, we decide who gets to do this by **voting**.

Voting is when people choose who they want to be their politician — their member of **parliament**. When the voting has finished, the people who are chosen go to London and work in a big building called Parliament. You might have seen this on the news, where there are often arguments and sometimes shouting.

"*What does law mean?*"

Laws are rules that should help everybody get along and decide when somebody is being mean. If people hurt others, the laws decide if they should be punished.

Punishment often means a **fine** — like a parking ticket if someone parks where they shouldn't. ***If people keep being mean*** and don't learn to behave, they might be sent to **prison**.

🗳 Vocabulary Box

Politics – the way people make decisions for the country.

Law – a rule that everyone must follow.

Vote – to choose who will make the laws.

Parliament – the building where laws are made in London.

Fine – money you must pay as a punishment.

Prison – a place where people are kept when they break serious laws.

Dice

GEOMETRY

*"What is **geometry**?"*

Geometry is a type of learning that is all about shapes. In geometry, we measure shapes so that we can learn important things about them.

LINES

Lines can be:

- **Horizontal** – level, flat lines.
- **Vertical** – straight up and down.
- **Diagonal** – slanted lines.

We measure how long a line is with a ruler, which is a straight piece of plastic or wood marked with centimetres.

■ SQUARES

Squares have four sides that are all the same length.

▭ RECTANGLES

Rectangles also have four sides — opposite sides are the same length.

◼ 2D AND 3D SHAPES

The shapes we have talked about so far are all flat. We call these *2-dimensional (2D).*

Some shapes are solid, not flat. These are *3-dimensional (3D).*

▲ CONES

Examples: traffic cones, ice cream cones.

🧊 CUBES

Made from six squares joined together.

A RUBIK'S CUBE

DICE

CYLINDERS

Examples: pipes, tubes, cans.

SPHERES

Examples: a ball, a globe.

THE EARTH

📘 VOCABULARY BOX

Geometry – the study of shapes and space.

Horizontal – flat, level line.

Vertical – straight up and down line.

Diagonal – slanted line.

2D (2-dimensional) – flat shapes.

3D (3-dimensional) – solid shapes.

Cube, **Cone**, **Cylinder**, **Sphere** – types of 3D shapes.

POOL BALLS

Flame

Wick

Made from

Wax

CANDLES

"What shall we talk about, Megan?"

"Candles!" she replies.

"What do you know about candles then?"

"Careful — you have to be careful with candles."

"Why?"

"*Because you can hurt yourself!*"

"Are candles dangerous?"

"Yes."

Candles are dangerous because they have a naked **flame**. This means they can burn you and set things alight.

Never leave candles unsupervised — the wind or a pet might knock them over.

Make sure they are **stable** — candles in glass jars are safer.

Lighting candles is tricky, and you can easily get a **burn**.

Keep candles **away** from **curtains** or anything that might catch fire.

Candles are made from **wax**, which is a kind of hard oil. Most candles use vegetable wax, but in the past, we used animal fat. Sometimes we also use **beeswax**.

🕯 VOCABULARY BOX

Flame – the bright, hot part of a fire.

Naked flame – a flame that is not covered or protected.

Wax – the solid material candles are made from.

Beeswax – wax made by bees, used for natural candles.

FOR SMALL BURNS IT HELPS TO RUN COLD WATER FROM THE TAP ONTO THE BURN FOR 1-2 MINUTES

DEXTER

WALKING TO COLLEGE

We like to walk into college.

If the weather is nice, or at least not raining, we walk **Dexter** from my house to my college.

"Yes," says Megan.

We try to walk even when it gets cold.

"*Cold?*" says Megan.

"*Yes — cold.* Then we might need a coat."

Even **Dexter** wears a coat when it's very cold. Megan waits outside with **Dexter** while Mum and Simon get ready.

Dexter has a **harness** and a **lead**. He also has a small collapsible bowl so he can have a drink of water.

"What else?" asks Simon.

"I think that is it," says Megan.

🎒 VOCABULARY BOX

College – a place where people go to study after school.

Weather – what the sky is like (sun, rain, cold, hot).

Harness – straps that go around a dog's body.

Lead – a rope or strap used for walking a dog.

THE MIND

"We can talk about the **mind** if you like?"

"Yeah, talk about **mind**."

"Ok. The best way is to start with a picture —
a **diagram**."

"*Why* have we got **diagram** word?"

"A **diagram** is a picture you use to explain
something."

"*Why* have we **explain**?"

"*Yes! Explain* means to teach somebody how
to understand something."

"*Why* do we have to **understand**?"

"You're just asking too many questions!"

Giggles.

A **diagram** is like a map — it's a picture that tells you something.

So, where were we... the **mind**.

Do you remember when we talked about the **five senses?**

We said we use our eyes to see, our ears to hear, our nose to smell, our tongue to taste, and our body to touch.

These are the **five senses.** We use them to learn about our world

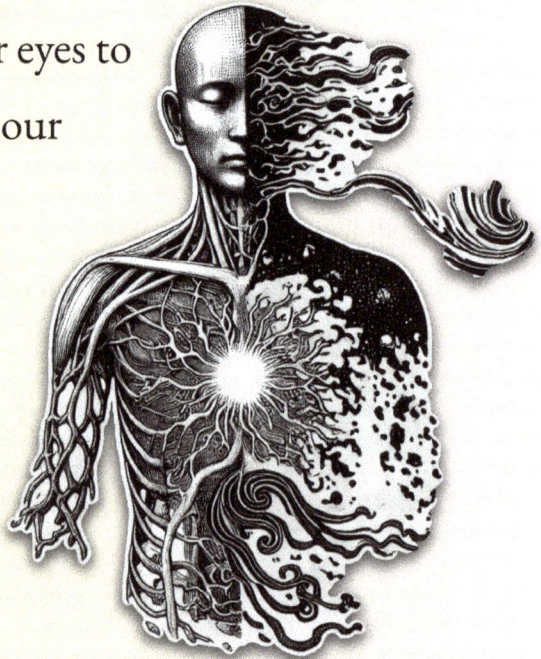

THE MIND

🧠 VOCABULARY BOX

Mind – the part of us that thinks and feels.

Diagram – a picture that explains something.

Explain – to teach or make something clear.

Understand – to know what something means.

Five senses – sight, hearing, smell, taste, and touch.

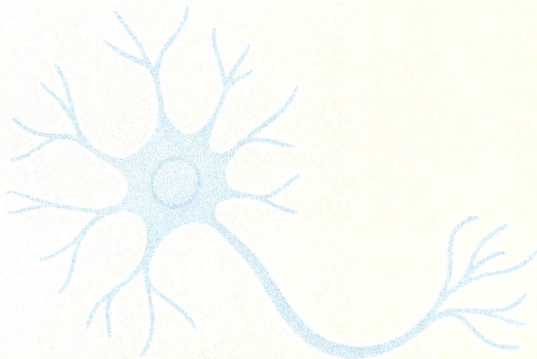

Want	Need
Another cup, water bottle, etc and already having a decent cup, water bottle etc. Fancy clothes, Expensive holidays Lots of attention. Expensive car. Big house.	Enough Food, Water, Warm and Dry Home, Some clothes, Some excitement, Some rest. Some attention. Occasional fun. Occasional challenges - learning.

☕ VOCABULARY BOX

Want – something you would like to have.

Need – something you must have.

Cupboard – a storage place with shelves and doors.

Overflowing – when something is so full it spills out.

WANT AND NEED

Megan **wants** a new cup.

But we already have *loads* of cups — our cupboards are full, even **overflowing!**

We don't have any *room*.

"So Megan — I know you want a cup, but do we really **need** any more cups?"

"I said *yes* — I **want** to."

Perfect. This is a lesson about **want** and **need.** You don't *really* **need** a new cup, do you?

"Yes!"

"Yes? *Really?* We have too many cups. How many cups do you have now, Megan?"

"One... or two."

"Really?"

We don't **need** any cups, *do we?*"

"No."

We have two shelves full of cups, and sometimes they even fall out because there is no room.

So what would happen if we all got new cups?

- One cup for *Megan.*
- One cup for *Simon.*
- One cup for *Mum.*
- One cup for *Grandad.*
- One cup for *Aunty Carol.*

That's **five** more cups! *Where* would we put them — *is there any room?*

"There's no room!"

"Exactly. So why don't you think about spending your money on something else?"

"Is that a good idea, or do you still want to buy a new cup?"

"I just want one because my old cup got broken!"

"Ah — so there won't be any more cups than before.

WAREHOUSE

PARCEL ON DOORSTEP

AMAZON

"What's that called?" Megan asked, pointing to the **Amazon app**.

"I think you already know about Amazon — even if you couldn't say its name."

"Maybe I can send it to Mum's, because I can't do it myself yet?"

"That's a good idea."

"If Mum is OK — yes or no — I don't know. But I'm sure Mum will say yes if she has the **money**."

"Yes."

"And this is a good idea, because ***it can be difficult to use Amazon safely.***"

"I'm thinking in my head — *I'm better!*" said Megan.

"Is that it then, are we finished?"

"Yes I do."

"No, it's 'Yes we are!'"

📦 VOCABULARY BOX

Amazon – a website and app where you can buy many things.

App – a program you use on a phone or tablet.

Safe – when something does not cause harm or problems.

Money – what you use to pay for things.

ANIMALS

"Well Megan, did you know most animals belong to one of five types?"

"*Types?*"

"Yes, most animals belong in one of these groups:

- **Fish** – they live in water and breathe through gills.

- **Amphibians** – animals that can live in both water and air.

- **Reptiles** – scaly animals that usually hatch from eggs.

- **Birds** – feathered animals that are born from eggs and most can fly.

- **Mammals** – animals born alive who drink their mother's milk."

🐟 FISH

Fish live in the sea, rivers, and lakes. They are born from soft eggs and breathe water.

"You know about fish, don't you?"

"Yes I do want fish!"

"Yes, you have fish with chips for dinner sometimes. That fish is called cod or hake. In Australia, it's sometimes shark!"

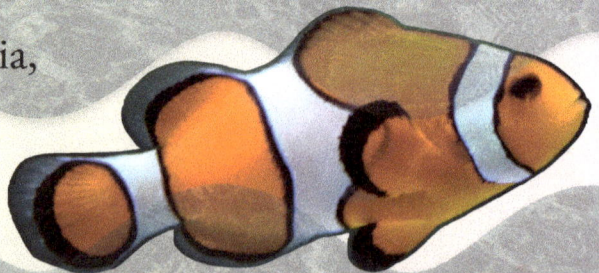

CLOWN FISH

🐸 AMPHIBIANS

"Am...fib...ians?"

"Yes, amphibians! These are creatures that can live and breathe in both water and air. Frogs, salamanders, and newts are amphibians."

NEWT

FROG

SHARK

2 REPTILES

Reptiles are animals that live on land and sometimes in water. They are born from eggs. This group includes snakes, lizards, turtles, crocodiles, and even dinosaurs!

SNAKE

CROCODILE

TURTLE

Birds are animals with wings, and most can fly. They are born from eggs.

"What birds do you know?"

"Seagulls, chickens, pigeons, and blackbirds..."

"What about the birds we see on the lake on our walk — quack, quack?"

"Ducks... and swans and geese."

PIGEONS

DUCKLING

ROBIN

BLACKBIRD

PELICANS

PARROTS

🐈 MAMMALS

Mammals give birth to living babies, who then drink milk.

We are mammals.

Cows are also mammals — they give us milk in the supermarket.

PANDA

Dogs are mammals too — when Dexter was a baby, he needed milk.

"Do you think that is enough?"

"Yes I do!"

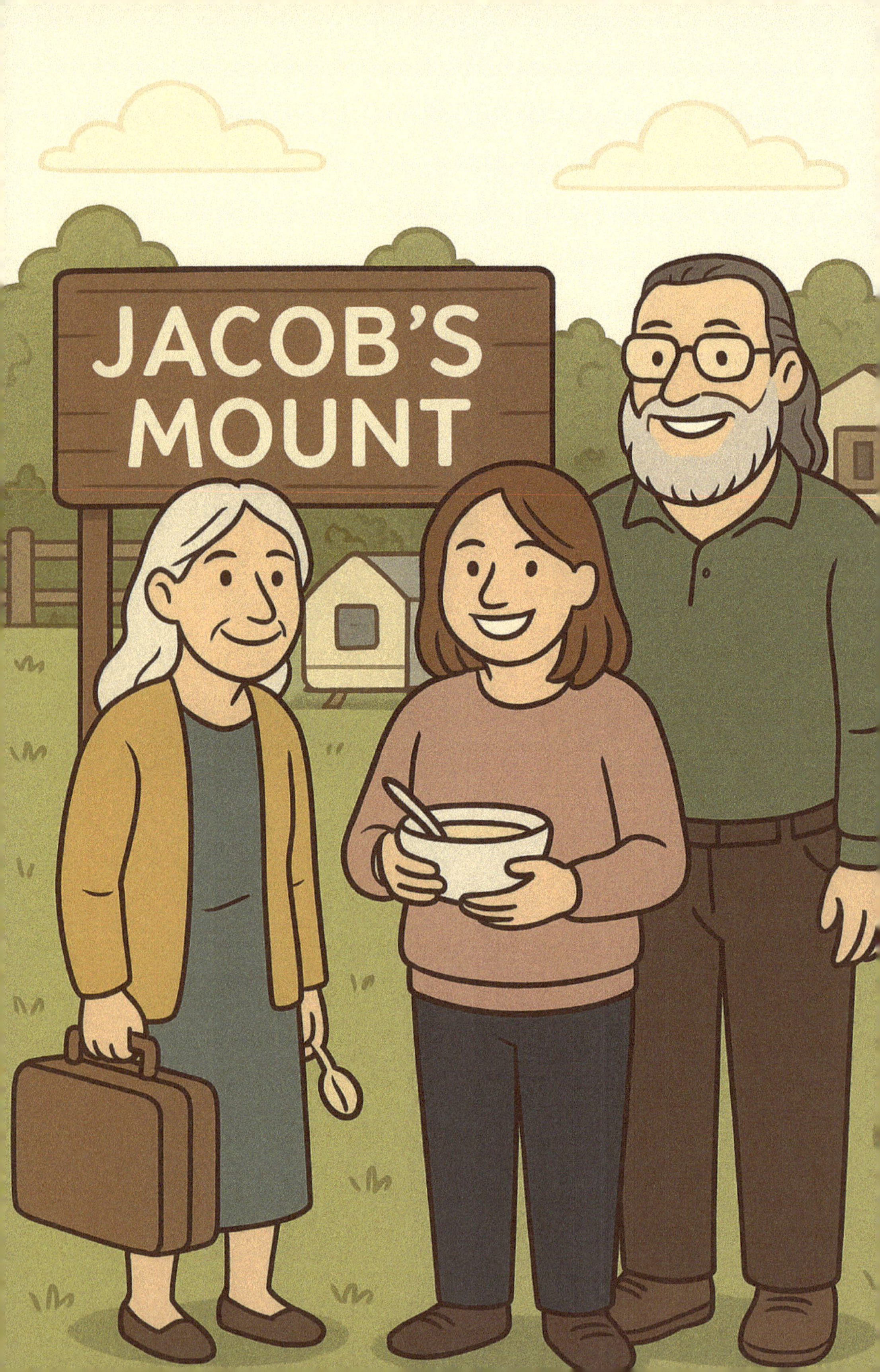
JACOB'S
MOUNT

PAT'S TEMPORARY ACCOMMODATION

Pat — *Simon's mum* — has been staying in **temporary accommodation.**

"What does *temporary* mean?"

Pat says, "It means it's not **permanent**. I am staying in a holiday **cottage** just until my new **bungalow** is ready for me to *move into*."

"I am going to Pat's new **house**. Pat says she's going to help me make mashed potato."

"Yes, like we used to — when we lived in Pickering."

"Are you getting your new house on WEDNESDAY?" asks Megan.

"No," replies Pat. "We are getting the keys on MONDAY."

"Hang on," says Simon. "This story is about temporary accommodation. So Pat, how has it been?"

"It's been very nice, but I am looking forward to moving into my new home."

"Are you excited, Megan?"

"**Yes I am**," she replies.

🏠 Vocabulary Box

Temporary – for a short time only.

Permanent – something that lasts and doesn't change.

Accommodation – a place where you stay or live.

Bungalow – a house with only one floor.

FOLDING LAUNDRY

DOING MY LAUNDRY

I have been learning how to do my own laundry.

We got a new washing machine, so I had to learn how to use this one.

First, I separate my laundry into **whites** and **colours.**

Then, I put in the **detergent pod** and a little **fabric conditioner.**

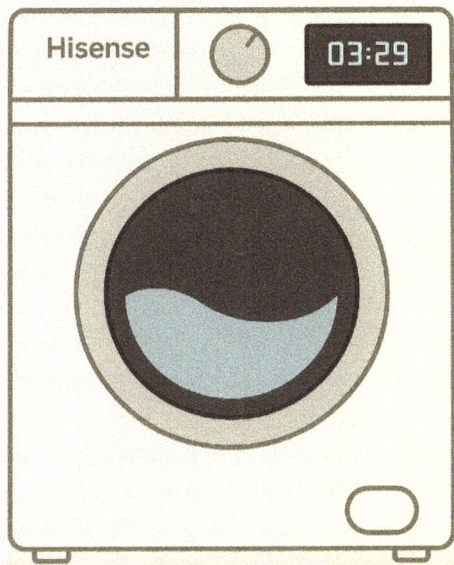

OUR NEW WASHING
MACHINE

"*So, Megan — can you do your laundry all by yourself?*" asks Simon.

"*Yes, I can do it **all by myself!***" says Megan.

I like to watch the washing spin round and round, and when it has finished, I put the wet clothes into the **dryer.**

When the dryer has finished, I take my clean clothes out, put them into a **basket,** and carry them upstairs. Then I put them away — most of the time!

The End

🟢 VOCABULARY BOX

Laundry – clothes and sheets that need to be washed.

Detergent pod – a small capsule with soap used for washing clothes.

Fabric conditioner – liquid that makes clothes soft and smell nice.

Dryer – a machine that dries clothes after they've been washed.

Basket – a container used to carry clean or dirty clothes.

🏠 TYPES OF HOUSES

Type of House	Description	Example in the UK
Cottage	Small, old house, often in the countryside.	Traditional cottages in the Cotswolds.
Bungalow	A house with only one floor.	Common in seaside towns and for retired people.
Flat / Apartment	One home inside a larger building.	City flats in London or Manchester.
Terrace House	A row of houses joined together.	Common in Victorian streets.
Semi-detached	Two houses joined side by side.	Suburban areas across the UK.
Detached	A house standing alone.	Larger homes in villages and towns.
Farmhouse	A house on farmland.	Yorkshire Dales farmhouses.
Mansion	A very large and grand house.	Historic estates like Chatsworth.
Castle	A fortified home of kings and lords.	Edinburgh Castle.

Vocabulary

Cottage – small, traditional house.

Bungalow – one-storey house.

Flat – home inside a bigger building.

Terrace – houses joined in a row.

Semi-detached – two houses joined together.

Detached – house by itself.

Farmhouse – house on a farm.

Mansion – very large house.

Castle – fortified historic home.

🐾 ANIMALS

Animals can be grouped into types, but it also helps to learn the names of common animals we see in daily life.

🐕 MAMMALS

Warm-blooded animals, born alive, drink their mother's milk.

Dog	Fox
Cat	Deer
Cow	Hedgehog
Horse	Whale
Sheep	Dolphin
Pig	Bat
Rabbit	

🐦 BIRDS

Feathered animals, most lay eggs and many can fly.

Robin	**Swan**
Blackbird	**Goose**
Pigeon	**Duck**
Seagull	**Owl**
Crow	**Sparrow**
Parrot	

🐟 FISH

Cold-blooded animals that live in water and breathe with gills.

Cod	**Carp**
Trout	**Shark**
Salmon	**Goldfish**

🐸 AMPHIBIANS

Live both in water and on land, usually begin life in water.

Frog
Toad
Newt

🐍 REPTILES

Scaly animals, most hatch from eggs.

Snake	**Turtle**
Lizard	**Crocodile**

📘 VOCABULARY BOX

Fish – animals that live in water and breathe through gills.

Amphibians – animals that can live in both water and air.

Reptiles – scaly animals that hatch from eggs.

Birds – animals with feathers and wings, usually born from eggs.

Mammals – animals that give birth to live young and feed them milk.

🕰 DAYS OF THE WEEK

The names of the days come from old languages and gods. Learning them helps us understand history as well as time.

Day	Meaning / Origin	Notes
Monday	"Moon's Day"	Named after the Moon.
Tuesday	From Tiw's Day	Tiw (or Tyr) was a Norse god of war.
Wednesday	From Woden's Day	Woden (Odin) was chief Norse god.
Thursday	"Thor's Day"	Thor was the Norse god of thunder.
Friday	From Frigg's Day	Frigg was a Norse goddess of love.
Saturday	From Saturn's Day	Saturn was a Roman god of time and farming.
Sunday	"Sun's Day"	Named after the Sun.

17 MONTHS OF THE YEAR

The calendar we use today comes from the Romans. Many month names are from Roman gods or Latin numbers.

VOCABULARY

Calendar – a way to measure time with days and months.

Festival – a special celebration.

Purification – making something clean or pure.

Fertility – the ability to grow new life.

Month – one twelfth of a year.

Month	Origin	Notes
January	Janus – Roman god of doors and beginnings	Faces both forwards and backwards.
February	From Februa, a Roman festival of purification	Time of cleansing.
March	Mars – Roman god of war	Soldiers prepared for battle in spring.
April	From Latin aperire = "to open"	Flowers open in spring.
May	Maia – Roman goddess of growth	Linked to plants and fertility.
June	Juno – Roman goddess of marriage	Time for weddings.

July	Named after Julius Caesar	Changed from Quintilis ("fifth month").
August	Named after Augustus Caesar	Changed from Sextilis ("sixth month").
September	"Seventh month" in Latin	But now the 9th month!
October	"Eighth month"	Now the 10th month.
November	"Ninth month"	Now the 11th month.
December	"Tenth month"	Now the 12th month.

🌍 THE PLANETS

The planets in our Solar System are named after Roman gods (except Earth). Each one is different.

Planet	Origin	Notes
Mercury	Roman messenger god	Smallest planet, fastest orbit around the sun.
Venus	Roman goddess of love	Brightest planet in our sky, sometimes called the "morning star."
Earth	From Old English eorðe (ground)	Our home, the only planet known with life.
Mars	Roman god of war	Red colour from iron dust.
Jupiter	King of the Roman gods	Largest planet, has a Great Red Spot storm.
Saturn	Roman god of time	Famous for its beautiful rings.
Uranus	Roman god of the sky	Spins on its side, very unusual.
Neptune	Roman god of the sea	Deep blue colour, farthest from the sun.

SHAPES

Shapes help us describe the world. Some are 2D (flat) and some are 3D (solid).

◆ 2D SHAPES (FLAT)

Shape	Description	Example
Circle	Round, no corners	Wheel, plate
Square	4 equal sides	Window, tile
Rectangle	2 long sides + 2 short sides	Door, book
Triangle	3 sides	Road sign, slice of pizza
Oval	Stretched circle	Egg, mirror
Hexagon	6 sides	Beehive honeycomb

◆ 3D SHAPES (SOLID)

Shape	Description	Example
Sphere	Ball shape	Football, globe
Cube	6 equal squares	Dice, box
Cylinder	Tube shape	Can, pipe
Cone	Pointed shape	Ice cream cone, traffic cone
Pyramid	Triangle sides + base	Egyptian pyramids

PYRAMID

🚗 TYPES OF TRANSPORT

Transport means the ways we travel from one place to another.

Type	Description	Example
Car	Most common everyday transport	Family car, taxi
Bus	Big vehicle carrying many people	Double-decker in London
Train	Runs on tracks across the country	InterCity trains, London Overground
Bicycle	Pedal-powered, two wheels	Cycling to school
Motorbike	Two wheels with an engine	Scooter, motorbike
Aeroplane	Flies in the sky, long distance	Flight from London to New York
Boat	Travels on water	Ferry across the Channel

Tram	Runs on tracks in cities	Manchester Metrolink
Underground / Tube	Trains under the ground	London Underground (since 1863)
Walking	Travelling on foot	Walking to college

📘 VOCABULARY

Transport – ways of getting from one place to another.

Vehicle – something that carries people or goods.

Journey – going from one place to another.

Passenger – person travelling in a vehicle.

Driver – person who controls a vehicle.

🚗 TYPES OF CAR BRANDS

Brand	Origin	Common Models
Ford	USA	Fiesta, Focus, Mondeo, Kuga
Vauxhall	UK/Germany	Corsa, Astra
Toyota	Japan	Yaris, Corolla, Prius
Nissan	Japan	Micra, Qashqai
BMW	Germany	3 Series, X5
Audi	Germany	A3, A4
Volkswagen	Germany	Golf, Polo
Honda	Japan	Civic, Jazz
Kia	South Korea	Sportage, Picanto
Hyundai	South Korea	i10, Tucson

🏠 ROOMS IN A HOUSE

Room	What it is for	Examples of things inside
Kitchen	Cooking and preparing food	Cooker, sink, fridge
Bathroom	Washing and cleaning	Bath, shower, toilet
Bedroom	Sleeping and resting	Bed, wardrobe, lamp
Living Room	Family space, relaxing	Sofa, TV, coffee table
Dining Room	Eating meals	Table, chairs
Hallway	Entrance space	Coats, shoes, stairs
Utility Room	Laundry and storage	Washing machine, dryer
Garage	Storage or car	Car, tools, bikes

WEATHER WORDS

Word	Meaning	Example
Sunny	Bright with sun	A hot summer day
Cloudy	Sky full of clouds	A grey morning
Rainy	Water falling from sky	Wet walk with umbrella
Snowy	Frozen flakes falling	Snowman in winter
Windy	Air blowing strongly	Flying a kite
Foggy	Thick mist in air	Hard to see on road
Stormy	Rain with thunder and lightning	Summer storm
Frosty	Ice on ground	Crunchy grass in morning
Hail	Small balls of ice from sky	Bouncing off cars
Rainbow	Colours after rain	Red, orange, yellow, green, blue, indigo, violet

👕 CLOTHES

Item	Use	Example
Coat	Keeps you warm outside	Winter coat
Jumper	Warm clothing for top half	Woolly jumper
Shirt	Smart clothing for top half	School uniform
T-shirt	Casual short-sleeved top	Holiday wear
Trousers	Covers both legs	Jeans, slacks
Skirt	Clothing for lower body	School skirt
Dress	One-piece outfit	Party dress
Shoes	Cover feet	Trainers, boots
Socks	Soft covering for feet	Ankle socks
Hat	Worn on head	Sunhat, woolly hat
Scarf	Worn round neck	Winter scarf
Gloves	Worn on hands	Mittens, winter gloves

👩‍⚕️ TYPES OF JOBS

Job	What they do	Where they work
Teacher	Helps people learn	School
Doctor	Treats sick people	Hospital, clinic
Nurse	Cares for patients	Hospital
Farmer	Grows food, raises animals	Farm
Police Officer	Keeps people safe	Streets, police station
Firefighter	Puts out fires	Fire station
Shop Assistant	Sells goods	Shop, supermarket
Builder	Builds houses and buildings	Construction site
Bus Driver	Drives buses	Roads, bus stations
Chef	Cooks food	Restaurant, café

🍎 FOOD GROUPS

Group	Examples	Why important
Fruit	Apples, bananas, oranges	Vitamins, energy
Vegetables	Carrots, peas, broccoli	Fibre, health
Meat & Fish	Chicken, beef, cod, salmon	Protein, strength
Dairy	Milk, cheese, yoghurt	Calcium for bones
Grains	Bread, rice, pasta	Energy, fibre
Sweets & Treats	Chocolate, cake, biscuits	Energy, but eat less!

💧 WATER

Source	Description	Example
Rain	Water falling from clouds	Showers in spring
River	Water flowing downhill	River Derwent
Lake	Still body of water	Lake Windermere
Reservoir	Man-made lake for storage	Ladybower Reservoir
Sea	Largest body of water	North Sea

Everyday Use	Why important
Drinking	Keeps us alive
Washing	Cleanliness and health
Cooking	Making food
Farming	Growing crops
Energy	Hydroelectric power

🔥 FUELS & SAFETY

Fuel	Example Use	Safety Tip
Gas	Cooker, heating	Smell for leaks
Electricity	Lights, chargers	Don't touch sockets
Oil	Heating, lamps	Keep stored safely
Wood	Fireplaces, stoves	Never leave unattended
Renewables	Solar, wind, water	Clean and safe

Fire Safety Rule	Why important
Don't leave flames alone	Prevents accidents
Keep away from curtains	Stops fire spreading
Use safe holders	Stops candles tipping
Ask an adult for help	Avoids burns

🗣 POLITENESS

Polite Behaviour	Example
Saying "please" and "thank you"	"Please may I have a drink?"
Waiting your turn	At the shop counter
Listening carefully	In class
Knocking before entering	Mum's bedroom door
Not gossiping	Keeping private things private

Rude Behaviour	Example
Interrupting	Talking over someone
Demanding	"Give me that!"
Ignoring people	Not answering
Gossiping	Talking about others

🔢 MATHS

Concept	Symbol	Example
Add	**+**	20 + 10 = 30
Subtract	**−**	40 − 35 = 5
Multiply	**✕**	4 × 10 = 40
Divide	**÷**	10 ÷ 2 = 5

Fraction	Percentage	Example
½	50%	Half a cake
¼	25%	Quarter of a pizza
⅓	33%	Third of a pie
1/10	10%	One coin in ten

Double	Answer	Half	Answer
2	4	2	1
5	10	10	5
8	16	20	10
12	24	100	50

VOCABULARY BOX

Percent (%) – a way of showing numbers out of one hundred.

100% – all of something, the whole thing.

50% – half of something.

0% – none of something.

Battery – the power that makes a phone or device work.

OUTER SPACE

Planet	Fun Fact
Mercury	Smallest, fastest around sun
Venus	Hottest planet
Earth	Our home
Mars	Red planet
Jupiter	Largest planet
Saturn	Famous rings
Uranus	Spins on side
Neptune	Deep blue

Sky Object	Seen when
Sun	Daytime
Moon	Night, or sometimes day
Stars	Night sky
Clouds	Any time
Planets	Bright dots in night sky

VOCABULARY BOX

Galaxy – a huge group of stars, planets, and space dust.

Star – a giant ball of burning gas, like the sun.

Planet – a round world that goes around a star.

Orbit – the path one thing takes as it goes around another.

Solar System – the sun, the planets, and their moons all together.

Milky Way – the name of our galaxy.

1. VERB TO BE

Tense	Forms
Present	I am, you are, he/she/it is, we are, you are, they are
Past	I was, you were, he/she/it was, we were, you were, they were
Future	I will be, you will be, he/she/it will be, we will be, you will be, they will be

2. VERB TO HAVE

Tense	Forms
Present	I have, you have, he/she/it has, we have, you have, they have
Past	I had, you had, he/she/it had, we had, you had, they had
Future	I will have, you will have, he/she/it will have, we will have, you will have, they will have

3. VERB TO GO

Tense	Forms
Present	I go, you go, he/she/it goes, we go, you go, they go
Past	I went, you went, he/she/it went, we went, you went, they went
Future	I will go, you will go, he/she/it will go, we will go, you will go, they will go

4. VERB TO DO

Tense	Forms
Present	I do, you do, he/she/it does, we do, you do, they do
Past	I did, you did, he/she/it did, we did, you did, they did
Future	I will do, you will do, he/she/it will do, we will do, you will do, they will do

VERBS - DOING WORDS

add	clean	give
ask	come	go
be	could	happen
become	decide	have
begin	do	hear
break	drink	help
bring	drive	keep
buy	explain	know
call	fall	learn
can	find	leave
carry	fly	like
change	get	live

look	show	understand
make	speak	use
mean	start	wait
move	stay	walk
need	stop	want
open	study	watch
pay	take	work
put	talk	write
read	teach	
remember	think	
say	travel	
see	try	
send	turn	

PURPOSE

The purpose of *All By Myself* is to continue the journey that began with *A Little Bit of Help* — to give Megan, and other young adults with similar learning challenges, a way to learn through stories that feel real and personal. Each chapter builds on familiar experiences, linking language to daily life and independence.

Since our first book, Megan's reading, vocabulary, and confidence have continued to grow. She now reads full sentences, understands longer ideas, and enjoys using her phone and calendar to plan her days. Her curiosity has deepened too — she asks more questions, makes new connections, and takes pride in finding words she knows in the world around her.

Our approach remains simple: learn through repetition, relevance, and enjoyment. Using real-world examples and vocabulary boxes helps to give meaning to new words and strengthens comprehension. Over time, each word learned becomes part of a larger picture — one that helps her see and understand the world with greater clarity.

Megan's progress shows that learning is not only about remembering; it's about seeing. When a pattern becomes visible — when letters, numbers, and ideas suddenly make sense — the world opens up.

If this book helps even one other learner, parent, or carer, then it has done its job. We plan to continue the series, adding new stories that celebrate confidence, independence, and discovery — a little bit more help, and a little more courage, every day.

ABOUT THE AUTHORS

This book continues the collaboration that began with *A Little Bit of Help (2024),* written as part of Megan's journey toward greater independence in reading and daily living. What began as short stories to practise language and comprehension soon became a shared project filled with laughter, learning, and discovery.

Megan's enthusiasm, questions, and sharp sense of humour have shaped every page. Simon's role has been to guide, listen, and translate those everyday conversations into stories that others might enjoy and learn from.

The series is designed for readers who, like Megan, learn best through relevance, repetition, and encouragement. Each title builds on the previous one, introducing new vocabulary, practical knowledge, and gentle confidence in self-expression.

Both authors live in North Yorkshire, where Dexter the dog still makes regular cameo appearances and new stories continue to unfold.

A LITTLE BIT OF HELP

OVERVIEW

A Little Bit of Help began as a personal project to help Megan, a young adult with learning disabilities, develop her reading and comprehension skills. Many educational books at her level were aimed at children, so this one was written especially for her — filled with stories drawn from daily life: tidying her room, going shopping, understanding time, and learning about colours, shapes, and emotions.

Each short chapter combines simple language, real experiences, and key vocabulary to make learning meaningful and enjoyable. The approach is practical and patient — teaching through relevance and repetition rather than abstract exercises.

The success of *A Little Bit of Help* was immediate. Megan's interest never wavered, and over time she mastered every concept in the book — from fractions to feelings. Her enthusiasm and constant chatter about "what we could write next" became the driving force behind its sequel, *All By Myself,* where she expresses her next big ambition: to learn to drive.

Lofty perhaps, but entirely sincere — and that's the heart of these books. They show that when learning is personal, hopeful, and connected to real life, progress isn't just possible — it's inevitable.

A LITTLE BIT OF HELP
BY MEGAN AND SIMON
A4 COLOUR EDITION – £9.99
AVAILABLE THROUGH AMAZON
ISBN: 9798334288362

AFTERWARD

www.ingramcontent.com/pod-product-compliance
Lightning Source LLC
Chambersburg PA
CBHW051259020426
42333CB00026B/3269

9 781068 431043